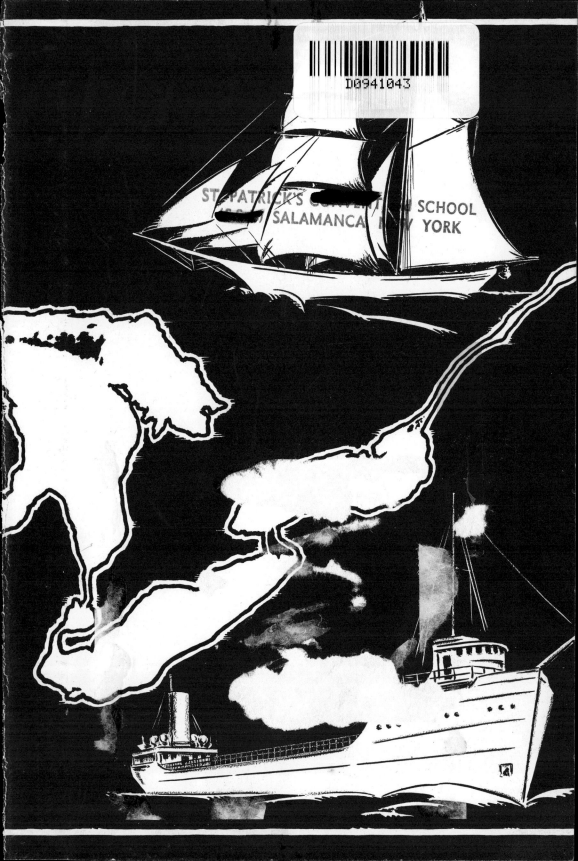

LET'S EXPLORE
THE GREAT LAKES

Stories and pictures of the
Great Lakes . . . .

F. RAYMOND ELMS
Author of
LET'S TAKE A TRIP
STORIES OF NEIGHBOR NATIONS
OUR UNITED STATES – HOW IT GREW
BUILDERS OF OUR NATION

—

ALBERT WHITMAN & COMPANY
CHICAGO, ILLINOIS

LET'S EXPLORE THE GREAT LAKES

To early French explorers and missionaries the Great Lakes were rightly named the Seas of Fresh Water.

Five huge lakes are linked together to form the Great Lakes: Lake Superior, Lake Michigan, Lake Huron, Lake Erie, and Lake Ontario. These lakes make up the largest expanse of fresh water in the world.

They are located in the north-central part of our country and lie between Canada and the United States. In part, the lakes help to form the International Boundary between the two countries.

At one time in the long history of this earth, a great ice sheet or glacier descended from the north. It spread over most of the area now occupied by the north-central states, covering it with a thick layer of ice.

As the glacier disappeared it scraped off the top soil in some regions. In other places it left the ground strewn with rocks, gravel, and coarse sand. In still other areas the glacier twisted and turned, scooping out the earth and forming great basins.

These became filled with water as the thick layer of ice slowly melted. In this manner were created the five Great Lakes and the hundreds and hundreds of smaller lakes that dot this part of our country.

Bold explorers and missionaries from France were the first white men to penetrate inland from the east. They made their way westward through the St. Lawrence River Valley and along the shores of lakes.

They came to the New World to explore, to trade, and to convert the natives to Christianity.

Before the Pilgrims had landed to establish their little colony at Plymouth, Frenchmen were busy exploring the Great Lakes area, trading with the Indians, and founding little settlements along the St. Lawrence River.

Samuel de Champlain has been called the Father of New France. For many years he worked hard trying to build a strong colony for France in the New World.

He was deeply religious and believed the natives could be converted to Christianity. Christianizing the Indians became an important part of French policy in America.

Champlain was responsible for bringing many of the first priests to the New World to work among the red men. He helped to establish missions. Wherever they were set up, these early missions were the first outposts of civilization.

In 1608, Champlain founded a small trading post at Quebec. The following year he was induced by the Algonquin Indians to join them in an attack against their old enemies, the Iroquois.

This expedition led Champlain to the lake in New York that now bears his name. He saw the waiting Iroquois lined along the water's edge and ordered his guns to be fired. A single volley put the astonished Indians to flight.

Their defeat made the Iroquois deadly enemies of the French. For many years their hostility forced the French to seek routes north of the Great Lakes in order to gain entrance to the interior of the country.

The French and Indian War brought to an end French expansion in the New World. By the peace treaty, signed in Paris in 1763, France agreed to cede to England all of Canada and the land east of the Mississippi River, except New Orleans.

Thus the Great Lakes, having been ruled by the French, came under English control. France was forced to abandon her dreams of a colonial empire in the New World.

The American Revolution was ended by the Treaty of Paris in 1783; the Great Lakes then became the boundary line separating England's possessions in America from the United States.

In 1909, the Boundary Waters Treaty was signed by Canada and the United States. By the terms of this treaty, both countries agreed to joint control of the five bodies of water. Ships may now move freely in all directions day and night.

To improve navigation on these lakes and to connect them with the Atlantic Ocean and the Mississippi River, canals, with locks, have been constructed.

The Great Lakes have played an important part in the development of the north-central states. Many industries flourish in this region.

Indian in birch bark canoe

LAKE SUPERIOR

Lake Superior, the largest of the Great Lakes, is the most northwesterly. It is the greatest single body of fresh water in the world.

It received its name from early French explorers who called it Lac Superieur, meaning the Upper Lake. It was so named to distinguish it from Lake Ontario at the lower end of the chain.

Etienne Brule was the first white man believed to have reached the shores of Lake Superior.

In 1608, when this young French explorer was only sixteen years old, he came with Champlain to the New World.

Two years later, Champlain sent him to live with the Indians. He was to learn their language, customs, and to acquaint himself with their country. When he returned to Quebec the following year, he was more like an Indian than a white man.

In 1612, he joined some Huron Indians on their way to their homes on Georgian Bay. While wandering about with the tribe, it is said he had his first glimpse of the deep blue waters of Lake Superior.

A small river of northern Wisconsin entering Lake Superior near its southwestern corner has been named for him.

Two Jesuit missionaries, Father Jogues and Father Raymbault, visited Sault Ste. Marie in 1641, giving the region its name.

Father Menard came here later; in the winter of 1660 and 1661 he ministered to the Indians living along the southern borders of Lake Superior.

Very early, two little mission stations were established in this region. One was at Sault Ste. Marie, the other at La Pointe, at the western end of the lake.

The mission at La Pointe was founded by Father Claude Allouez. He followed Father Menard into the Lake Superior country.

These missions were meeting places for priests, fur traders, explorers, and Indians. Many tales were told by Indians about copper mines and a great river to the south.

When these stories made their way back to the settlements, more and more men were inspired to explore the area.

Lake Superior is crescent-like in shape. It is six hundred and two feet above sea level, at the highest elevation of all the Great Lakes. From east to west it is over three hundred and

fifty miles long and its greatest breadth is about one hundred and sixty miles.

The Canadian Province of Ontario borders the lake on the north and east, while Minnesota forms the western boundary. Northern Wisconsin and Michigan's Upper Peninsula form its southern shoreline.

Winters in the Lake Superior area are very cold. They start early and often last late into the spring. The lake never freezes over completely, due to its great depth. But huge mounds of ice pile up in shallow water along shorelines; and choke bays and harbors around the lake.

Several large bays indent the shoreline. Along the northern or Canadian side are Thunder Bay, Black, Nipigon, and Heron Bays. They all form fine harbors for many ships during the months navigation is possible on the lake. Whitefish, Chequamegon and Keweenaw Bays are found along the southern shoreline.

Samuel de Champlain

High cliffs rise sharply from the water along the Canadian shore. They range from about three hundred to over one thousand feet high.

This shoreline is very picturesque, and affords some of the boldest and most beautiful scenery in the Great Lakes region. Much of the country is covered with dense forests of pine.

For the most part, the southern shore of Lake Superior is low, except for occasional ridges. The most outstanding feature here is a rock formation east of Munising, Michigan.

Pictured Rocks is a wall of colorful red sandstone that rises to a height of about three hundred feet. It is broken by many caverns and projections carved into fantastic shapes by high winds and pounding waves. This strange rock wall is one of the natural beauty sights of our country.

More than two hundred rivers empty their waters into Lake Superior. A few of the larger, entering from the north, are the St. Louis, Pigeon, Kaministikwia, Nipigon, Pic, White, and Michipicoten Rivers. No rivers of any great size flow into the lake from the south.

Islands rise from the water along both shores. Near the southern shore they are small. But some found on the north are of considerable size. Of these, Isle Royale is the largest.

Northwest of Copper Harbor, Michigan, and near the Canadian border, Isle Royale is almost forty-five miles long and about nine miles at its greatest width.

Its shore is rugged and deeply indented. Sea caves, rocky beaches and rock towers add to its wild beauty.

The Indians knew about and mined the copper deposits on the island. Some of their copper pits, said to be six hundred to eight hundred years old, can still be seen.

It has been said that rumors of these deposits were brought to the attention of Benjamin Franklin. At the time, he was attending a meeting in Paris, France where the International Boundary was being laid out. He insisted that the valuable island must become part of the new United States, and this was done. It is now part of Michigan.

Isle Royale has been set aside as a National Park and remains a wilderness. For visitors, there are lodges which are reached by trail and small boats.

This island is a combination of forest, open glades, marshes, inland lakes of which there are about thirty. Both marshes and lakes are the haunts of moose. In fact, it is a sanctuary for all wildlife.

Other large islands in Lake Superior are Isle St. Ignace, Pic, Slate, Simpson, Michipicoten, and Apostle Islands.

Split Rock Lighthouse—Lake Superior

Copper Mine

The Apostle Islands cluster around a large peninsula on the Wisconsin shore east of Superior. They received their name from French Jesuit priests who believed there were only twelve islands. But there are twenty or more in the group.

The land surrounding the lake is rich in deposits of copper, iron ore, nickel, and other metals.

A Frenchman named Louis Denis, Sieur de la Ronde, hoped to develop trade in copper. To do this he needed ships; so at Sault Ste. Marie, in 1734, he built the first sailing ship to appear on Lake Superior. He made plans to build a second ship, larger than the first, but he died before his dream was realized.

Over a hundred years later, in 1837, a survey was made in the Upper Peninsula of Michigan and copper was found. When the official report was made public, men clamored for passage to this part of the country.

Dreams of finding great fortunes filled their heads. With their worldly possessions strapped on their backs, these adventurers set out. Many of them staked out claims, only to abandon them a short time later. Some prospectors died from starvation, while others froze to death during the long, cold winter.

The Keweenaw Peninsula, a spur-shaped piece of land that juts out into the lake, is known as the Copper Country. About one-seventh of the world's copper is mined every year in this region.

Among the first copper towns to appear on Lake Superior were Eagle River and Copper Harbor. Calumet, Hancock, Houghton, and other towns soon appeared when the Copper Rush was at its height.

The mines in this region are the only important copper mines east of the Mississippi River, these are extremely deep.

KEWEENAW PENINSULA

On September 19, 1844, a party of surveyors discovered iron ore. Unlike the great depth at which copper had to be mined, the surveyors found outcroppings of iron ore on the surface of the ground.

The first shipment of reddish-black ore from the Lake Superior country was made in six barrels on July 7, 1852. It was brought by Indian trail and wagon to the shore of the lake. Here it was loaded onto a ship.

When the ship reached Sault Ste. Marie the barrels had to be portaged around the falls of the St. Mary's River, because no locks had been built.

Yet three years later, on August 14, 1855, the brig Columbia passed through the American Canal and Lock. Its cargo of one hundred and thirty-two tons was the first shipment of iron ore to pass through the lock.

Some of the greatest iron ore mines in the world are in Minnesota and Michigan. Of the great iron ranges, the Mesabi, Cuyuna, Gogebic, and Vermilion, the Mesabi produces the greatest amount of ore.

This high quality ore lies close to the earth's surface and in places in Northern Minnesota it is mined from open pits.

There is much commerce on Lake Superior. Shipping lanes cross the lake in all directions, but the main routes are from the western end of the lake to the locks at Sault Ste. Marie.

Of the cargoes carried, iron ore is the most important. Eastbound, it is the chief product carried by ships, while westbound, coal is the main cargo.

The most common type of ship now sailing the lake is the great steel ore carrier. It is very long, sometimes more than 600 feet, with cabins at its bow and stern. Between them are long rows of covered openings.

Iron Ore Docks

Duluth, Minnesota

These openings are called hatches. Iron ore is poured into the hatches from huge spouts set on specially built docks. When fully loaded, the carrier rides very low in the water.

Lake Superior has been the scene of many disasters. Fortunes in copper, iron ore, machinery, coal, and limestone rest beneath the busy shipping lanes of the lake.

Ships have sailed out of harbors never to be seen or heard from again. Such was the case of the "Bannockburn."

The "Bannockburn" left Duluth on her way to Whitefish Bay. She passed Keweenaw Point, but never reached her destination. Only one trace of the freighter or any of her crew was ever found.

About a year and a half after the ship disappeared, an oar was uncovered from a mass of driftwood that had collected on the wild south shore of the lake. Beneath a tattered piece of canvas around the handle of the oar was the roughly carved name "Bannockburn."

Some of the larger and more important cities on the American shore of the lake are Duluth, Minnesota, Superior and Ashland, Wisconsin, and Marquette, Michigan. On the Canadian side, Fort William and Port Arthur, Ontario, are the largest cities.

Superior and Duluth are the two biggest ports on the lake. These cities are situated at the extreme western end of the lake. They lie on opposite sides of a bay which affords both cities an excellent harbor.

Comparatively close by are the great iron ore mines of the region, extensive forests, and rich farm lands. Farms of this area produce huge quantities of wheat.

Great amounts of iron ore and lumber, wheat, and flour are shipped from these ports each year.

Pictured Rocks

Fort William, Ontario, is at the head of Canadian navigation on Lake Superior. It is situated at the mouth of the Kaministikwia River. Port Arthur lies only a short distance east of Fort William. The two Canadian cities are shipping centers and important grain ports.

Fishing is an important industry on the lake which is well stocked with whitefish, trout, and sturgeon. Fish caught in Superior's deep, cold waters are among the best in all the Great Lakes. Throughout the Middle West, Lake Superior whitefish are greatly esteemed.

The lake is about twenty-two feet higher than its eastern neighbor, Lake Huron. They are connected by the St. Marys River.

The river is about sixty-three miles long, but its Falls make it useless as a commercial waterway. In order that ships might pass from one lake to the other, canals with locks had to be constructed around the Falls.

The first canal was built on the Canadian side by the Northwest Fur Company in 1797 and 1798. It was very small, but helped to serve fur traders operating in the region. It was destroyed by the Americans in the War of 1812.

Canals have now been built on both sides of the St. Marys River. Commonly known as the Soo Canals, the waterway consists of five canals with locks. There is only one canal and lock on the Canadian side of the river. The other four are on the American side.

The Canadian Canal with lock was started in 1888 and completed in 1895. The canal is one hundred and fifty feet wide and twenty-five feet deep. It has **one lock** nine hundred feet long and sixty feet wide with a lift of eighteen feet.

The first American Canal with lock was completed in 1855.

Docks at Superior

On June 18 of that year Captain Jack Wilson took the side-wheeler steamship "Illinois" through the new canal for the first passage of any vessel into Lake Superior.

The first canal on the American side was built by the State of Michigan. It continued to be operated by Michigan until 1881, when it was taken over by the government of the United States.

The four American Canals lie side by side. Each has one lock.

As the number of ships increased, the canals and locks were enlarged and improved. Of the four American Canals the MacArthur is the newest.

In 1943, the MacArthur replaced the old Weitzel lock. It is now the deepest of the American locks. It is eight hundred feet long and eighty feet wide.

Old Sidewheel Steamer

The MacArthur Lock

The five Canals form the first link in the chain of Great Lakes.

For many years, larger ships traveling between Lake Superior and Lake Huron used the Canadian Canal. Today the larger and deeper American Canals enable even the biggest lake ships to pass through into Lake Huron.

LAKE MICHIGAN

Lake Michigan is the only one of the Great Lakes lying wholly within the borders of the United States.

It is the third largest of the lakes, being only slightly smaller than Lake Huron. Its elevation is about five hundred and eighty feet above sea level. From north to south it is over three hundred miles long, and at its greatest width about one hundred and eighteen miles wide.

Lake Michigan stretches southward, dividing the state into two sections, the Upper and Lower Peninsulas.

On the north it is bounded by the Upper Peninsula, while its eastern shores are bounded by the Lower Peninsula. Indiana borders the lake on the south and Illinois and Wisconsin form its western boundary.

The first white man to visit Lake Michigan was the French explorer, Jean Nicolet. He came to Canada with Champlain and spent about two years living with the Indians, learning their language, customs, and crafts.

In 1634 he started out to explore the country. Like many of the early explorers, Nicolet was looking for a route to the Orient.

He set out in a single large canoe with seven Indians. They paddled from Georgian Bay through the Straits of Mackinac and on into Lake Michigan.

Skirting the west coast they arrived in the northwestern region of the lake now known as Green Bay.

Here Nicolet prepared to land and meet the natives. Before going ashore he arrayed himself in an elaborate Oriental robe.

[24]

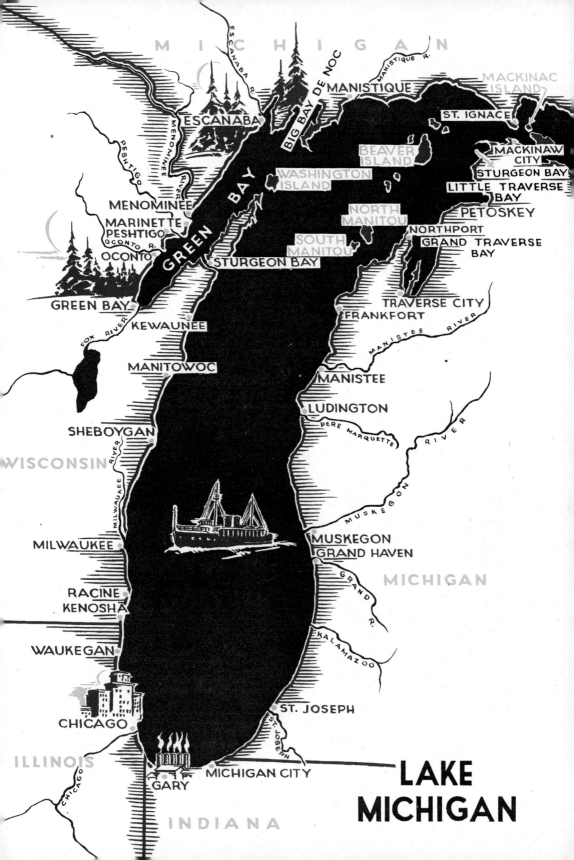

MICHIGAN

ESCANABA R.

MANISTIQUE R.

MICHIGAN

MACKINAC ISLAND

MANISTIQUE

BIG BAY DE NOC

ST. IGNACE

ESCANABA

MACKINAW CITY

BEAVER ISLAND

STURGEON BAY

WASHINGTON ISLAND

LITTLE TRAVERSE BAY

MENOMINEE

NORTH MANITOU

PETOSKEY

MENOMINEE RIVER

MARINETTE
PESHTIGO
OCONTO R.

SOUTH MANITOU

NORTHPORT
GRAND TRAVERSE BAY

PESHTIGO R.

OCONTO

STURGEON BAY

GREEN BAY

TRAVERSE CITY

GREEN BAY

FRANKFORT

FOX RIVER

KEWAUNEE

MANISTEE RIVER

MANITOWOC

MANISTEE

LUDINGTON

SHEBOYGAN

PERE MARQUETTE RIVER

WISCONSIN

SHEBOYGAN RIVER

MILWAUKEE RIVER

MUSKEGON RIVER

MILWAUKEE

MUSKEGON
GRAND HAVEN

MICHIGAN

GRAND R.

RACINE
KENOSHA

WAUKEGAN

KALAMAZOO R.

ST. JOSEPH

CHICAGO

ST. JOSEPH R.

ILLINOIS

CHICAGO R.

GARY

MICHIGAN CITY

INDIANA

LAKE MICHIGAN

Instead of finding the Orientals that he had expected, he was greeted by friendly Winnebago Indians. He was well received, greatly admired, and was treated like a god.

Before returning to Canada, Nicolet made a treaty of alliance with the Indians. He prepared the way on Lake Michigan for the missionaries, explorers, and traders who were to follow.

Father Jacques Marquette, a Jesuit missionary, was sent to the small mission at Sault Ste. Marie in 1668. In 1671 he founded a new mission at St. Ignace.

Joliet and Marquette, with a small party in two birch bark canoes, set out from St. Ignace. Entering Green Bay they followed the shore until they reached the outlet of Fox River. They crossed the area that is now Wisconsin by way of the Fox and Wisconsin Rivers.

On June 17, 1673, they paddled into the broad waters of the Mississippi River. They continued south along its west bank until they were convinced the Mississippi emptied into the Gulf of Mexico.

Father Jacques Marquette

They returned along its east bank, coming to the Illinois River. Slowly they made their way back to the little mission of St. Francis Xavier, near Green Bay. Here they stopped for the winter.

The following spring, Joliet started out for Canada alone because Marquette was ill and had to remain behind.

Marquette was greatly loved by the Indians. He continued with his work, revisiting the Indians of the Illinois area.

His strength began to fail and he was anxious to return to his mission at St. Ignace. In May, 1675, he reached the mouth of the Pere Marquette River at Ludington, Michigan, where he died.

Four years later Robert Cavelier, Sieur de La Salle, led a trading expedition into the Great Lakes. He and

Robert Cavelier, Sieur de La Salle

thirty-four other men started on August 7, 1679, in a tiny sailing ship, the "Griffon."

The ship sailed from the Niagara River. Indians along the shore were so astonished by the strange vessel that they called it the Great White Bird.

La Salle and his men crossed Lake Erie to its western end, sailed up a long river and into a wide body of water which he named Lake St. Clair. Then he reached another river, giving it the same name.

Once in Lake Huron, the "Griffon" sailed north to the Straits of Mackinac and St. Ignace. Here the party stopped to rest.

By September 3 the "Griffon" had entered Lake Michigan.

La Salle finally cast anchor in what is now Green Bay, always following the west shoreline.

His agents, sent out the year before, were waiting with

[27]

an abundance of furs. The little ship was soon loaded and ready to return to Niagara.

La Salle decided to remain to explore the region and gave orders for his ship to sail back for him in the spring.

The "Griffon" weighed anchor on September 18, 1679. A short time after the ship set sail, a storm arose which raged for four days. During the gale the "Griffon" was lost and was never heard from again.

The disappearance of La Salle's ship was the first of a long series of disasters on Lake Michigan.

On September 8, 1860, the "Lady Elgin" was on a return trip to Milwaukee from an excursion to Chicago. She was about twenty miles on her course when a storm arose and heavy fog settled over the water.

Meantime the schooner "Augusta," loaded with lumber, was heading for Chicago. Either the schooner could not see the blurred riding lights of the "Lady Elgin" or misjudged her distance from the excursion ship. For she drove straight across the path of the northbound vessel.

The ships met and the sharp prow of the "Augusta" hit the "Lady Elgin" amidships. They soon drew apart, the lumber schooner proceeding on her course to Chicago.

In a few minutes the "Lady Elgin" filled with water and foundered. She sank so quickly that only two lifeboats were able to get away.

The master of the ill-fated vessel was the same Captain Jack Wilson, who, five years earlier had sailed the side-wheeler "Illinois" through the newly completed Soo Locks.

On November 25, 1913, in a rising storm, the "Rouse Simmons" set out from Manistique. She was carrying a cargo of Christmas trees, bound for Chicago.

Chicago, Illinois

Coast Guard Patrol Boat

The following day the Coast Guard at Sturgeon Bay, while on patrol, saw a schooner whose decks were covered with Christmas trees. She was flying distress signals.

In the wild waters the guardsmen were unable to launch their boat, but reported the "Simmons" to the Coast Guard Station south at Kewaunee, Wisconsin.

In the larger boat launched from the Kewaunee Station the Coast Guard searched everywhere for the "Rouse Simmons," fighting strong winds, high seas and heavy snow. But she had vanished. She was never seen again.

When the following spring rolled around, stories were told of Christmas trees fouling fishermen's nets along the Wisconsin shore.

Coast Guard stations have been established on the Great Lakes. The crews keep an ever-watchful eye on the water, bringing help to those in distress.

The eastern shore of the lake is sandy. Beautiful beaches with swimming, boating, and other forms of recreation attract visitors. High sandy bluffs rising from the beaches are often covered with trees and shrubs.

Inland from the shore is a mixed farming region. A narrow strip of land thirty miles deep, running the full length of the Lower Peninsula, is well adapted to the raising of fruit.

This is the famous fruit belt of Michigan. Apples, peaches, pears, plums, cherries, grapes, and berries are raised in great quantities.

More cherries are raised in Michigan than anywhere else in America. The cherry country is around Traverse City and Northport. It has been called the Capital of Cherryland.

To the south along the Indiana shoreline is a district of sandy ridges called the Sand Dunes. Some of these sand ridges are as high as four hundred feet. It has become a

Sand Dunes

popular recreation area. Many summer and year-round homes are found here.

Great steel mills are also located on this shore, Gary, Indiana being an important center for this industry.

Along the Wisconsin side, farming and dairying are very important industries.

For the most part, the rivers emptying into Lake Michigan are small. Those of the Upper Peninsula are faster flowing and more turbulent than the rivers of the Lower Peninsula.

From the Upper Peninsula the Menominee, Escanaba, Whitefish, and Manistique rivers are the largest. Flowing into the lake from the east coast are the Manistee, Muskegon, Grand, Kalamazoo, Paw Paw, Pere Marquette, and St. Joseph rivers. From the western shore, the Fox, Milwaukee, Oconto, and Peshtigo rivers are the largest. The Chicago River flows out of the lake.

The two largest rivers are the Menominee and the Fox. Both discharge their waters into Green Bay.

Green Bay is the largest bay of the lake. It is in the northwestern corner, about one hundred miles long and from ten to twenty miles wide. A few of the other bays are Big Bay de Noc, Little Bay de Noc, Sturgeon Bay, Little Traverse Bay, and Grand Traverse Bay.

There are no islands in the southern half of Lake Michigan. But many are located in the upper region: Washington, Beaver, North and South Manitou, High, Hog, North and South Fox, and Garden Islands.

Eighteen seventy-one was the year of two great fires in the Lake Michigan area: the Chicago fire in Illinois and the Peshtigo fire in northeastern Wisconsin.

Flames swept through Chicago quickly, leveling the whole

Unloading ore at Gary, Indiana

Old Water Tower—Chicago

city north of the river. The only building to survive the blaze is said to be the Old Water Tower.

Many citizens living within reach of the lake buried valuables in their yards or what belongings they could carry and dashed to the water's edge for protection. Boats were also pressed into service to take people out on the water, away from the terrific heat of the fire.

The Peshtigo fire burned great swaths across parts of Wisconsin and Michigan. Wherever possible, people sought refuge at the water front. Crowded steamers and boats of all kinds steered for the open water, away from the inferno on land.

Much shipping moves up and down Lake Michigan. Huge quantities of iron ore from Lake Superior ports are shipped to the steel mills at Gary, Indiana, and other points along the southern shore. Large amounts of grain come to Chicago.

Some other important cargoes are copper, machinery, coal, wood, paper pulp, and food products.

To save the long trip around the lower end of Lake Michigan, a system of ferries has been established. They carry passengers, automobiles and freight cars; and operate between Milwaukee, Manitowoc, Kewaunee, Menominee, and Manistique on the western shore and Muskegon, Ludington, and Frankfort on the eastern shore.

Huge car ferries transport tourists and their cars from the northern tip of the Lower Peninsula at Mackinaw City across the Straits of Mackinac to St. Ignace on the Upper Peninsula.

In summer beautiful, large passenger ships make scheduled cruises on the Great Lakes. They stop at the Soo and other points of interest. These ships are like floating hotels; and offer their passengers many forms of recreation and the comforts of large ocean liners.

Car Ferry

North of Chicago, on the western shore of Lake Michigan is the United States Naval Training Center, the world's largest naval training station. Thousands of sailors of World War I and World War II received their training here, although the base is nearly a thousand miles from salt water.

During World War II, the "Wolverine," and her sister ship, the "Sable," were stationed on Lake Michigan. Both of these ships were aircraft carriers and had been converted to flat-tops from large lake passenger ships. They were used for training fliers.

Some of the larger cities on Lake Michigan in the Upper Peninsula are Menominee, Escanaba, and Manistique. Along the Lower Peninsula are Petoskey, Traverse City, Manistee, Ludington, Muskegon, Grand Haven, and St. Joseph. Gary is the chief Indiana port, and two Illinois coast cities are Chicago and Waukegan.

Along the Wisconsin coast, Kenosha, Racine, Milwaukee, Sheboygan, Manitowoc, Sturgeon Bay, Green Bay, and Marinette are the most important.

The Chicago Canal System, starting at the southwestern part of the lake, connects Lake Michigan with the Mississippi River.

A canal, the Illinois-Michigan Canal, was completed in 1848 from the Chicago River southwest to the Illinois River just below La Salle, Illinois. It is no longer used, being too narrow for the needs of the time.

In 1900, the Chicago Drainage Canal, later called the Chicago Sanitary and Ship Canal, was completed. This connects the south branch of the Chicago River with the Des Plaines River at Lockport and provides a navigable channel twenty-one feet deep.

Tower—United States Naval Training Center

Construction of the Canal was started in 1892 and was finally completed on January 2, 1900. On that day, the bulkhead was cut through and the Chicago River was turned backward in its course.

Water flowing out of Lake Michigan finds it way through this Canal and the Des Plaines River to the Illinois River. At a point above the city of Alton, the Illinois River finally joins the Mississippi.

Lake Michigan has two of the seven largest Great Lakes ports. These are Chicago and Milwaukee. Both cities are great industrial centers.

Chicago now occupies the site that at one time was Fort Dearborn, built in 1803 and named for General Henry Dearborn.

Milwaukee, Wisconsin

Fishing Boat

It is the most important port on Lake Michigan. Because of its favorable location, Chicago has become one of the world's greatest industrial centers. Raw materials can be brought to the city's factories by air, water, railroad, and highway, to be converted into manufactured products.

Chicago is an important iron and steel manufacturing center and in meat packing, the city leads the world.

Fishing in Lake Michigan is a very important industry. Whitefish, lake trout, sturgeon, pickerel, herring, and perch being chief among the catch.

Passage from Lake Michigan to Lake Huron is made by way of the Straits of Mackinac. This deep body of water is about forty-eight miles long and it has a minimum width of about six miles. The Straits are the second link in the chain of the five Great Lakes.

LAKE HURON

Lake Huron was the first of the five Great Lakes to be discovered by the French. Although Champlain probably was not the first white man to see any of the lakes, he was the first to record the fact for history.

On one of his trips from France he brought along several priests. One of them was Father Joseph Le Caron. The party came to the little settlement of Quebec in 1615.

Both men had the same destination in mind. But Father Le Caron was very anxious to start his work as a missionary. Instead of waiting with Champlain he and a few followers set out from Montreal a week ahead of Champlain.

Father Le Caron reached the shore of Lake Huron, and having only one thought in mind, he did not linger. He continued on his way until he came to the little Huron Indian village of Carhagouha, where he was to begin his work.

Champlain followed close behind Father Le Caron. On this expedition he took Etienne Brule with him. Brule had spent quite a considerable time living with the Indians and was valuable as an interpreter.

Champlain and his men reached Lake Huron by way of a northern route. They traveled up the Ottawa River, reaching Lake Nipissing by a portage path through the wilderness. They continued to paddle across Lake Nipissing until they came to the French River. Then they floated down this river to its mouth in Georgian Bay, the great arm of Lake Huron.

On July 28, 1615, Samuel de Champlain and his followers paddled out of the French River into the clear blue waters of Georgian Bay.

When he beheld the beautiful sight for the first time he called it "La Mer Douce," the Freshwater Sea. At a later date the lake was renamed Huron, for the Huron Indians who lived along the shore.

Champlain and his followers continued on their way, and finally reached the little village of Carhagouha. Here they were warmly greeted by Father Le Caron.

Champlain opened up a route of travel that was to be traveled for many years. It was used by priests, fur traders, and explorers who came after him into the region.

Furs and fur trading very early became an important industry of this part of the country. For about two centuries fur trading dominated the life of the Lake Huron district.

The area that is now the State of Michigan was at one time covered by huge forests. Many wild animals roamed

Champlain greeted by Father Le Caron

Old Trading Post

about and it was one of the great fur-bearing regions of the Old Northwest.

During this era the little settlements of Detroit and Mackinac were important centers for trading. Traders met in these villages. Indians brought in skins of the animals they had trapped, to exchange for articles the traders had to offer.

Lake Huron is the second largest of the five Great Lakes. In the chain of lakes it is situated between Lake Michigan and Lake Erie.

It lies at an elevation of five hundred and eighty feet above sea level. Its elevation is about the same as that of Lake Michigan, but it is about twenty-two feet lower than Lake Superior.

The northern and eastern boundaries of the lake are formed by the Canadian province of Ontario. On the south it is bounded by Michigan and part of Ontario; and Michigan borders it on the west.

Some of the larger rivers, finding their way into Lake Huron from the Canadian shore are the Mississagi, Wanapitei, French, Maganetawan, Saugeen, and Maitland rivers.

The four most important flowing into Lake Huron from the Michigan shore are the Cheboygan, Au Sable, Thunder Bay; and the Saginaw, with its four tributaries, the Shiawassee, Cass, Flint, and Tittabawassee rivers.

At one time these rivers played an important role in the development of the region. Logs from dense inland forests were floated down these waterways to sawmills where they were converted into lumber. Today the rivers are seldom used to move logs.

During the 1880's the lumbering industry was at its peak. Saginaw, Alpena, Cheboygan, and Bay City were all bustling mill towns. Both sides of the rivers on which towns were situated were spaced with sawmills for many miles. Great piles of drying lumber lined both shores.

A sharp smell of resin from sawdust piles greeted those entering the towns. When the wind came from the land, the biting smell drifted out over the water.

In spring, when lumbermen, in their gay plaid jackets and tasseled caps, swarmed in from their camps, the mill towns were beehives of activity and very colorful.

Fire was always a great hazard for the towns. Frame buildings, wooden sidewalks, and cliffs of lumber in drying yards could quickly be turned into seas of flames that sometimes enveloped an entire town.

Nearly every town had its fires; some towns had a series of them.

Sawmill

Loading Limestone at Alpena

When lumbering declined, the towns had to seek other means of livelihood. Limestone was discovered at the edge of Alpena. It proved to be one of the richest deposits of limestone in our country.

The manufacturing of cement was started. Now, Alpena ships Portland cement to all ports on the Great Lakes, for use in the construction of highways and many other purposes. Alpena is one of the chief loading points for limestone.

The limestone trade has grown until it has developed into one of the important cargoes carried by Great Lakes freighters.

Lake Huron's shores are low except along the southeastern coast. Here rough cliffs rise to a height of around one hundred and fifty feet. Much of the territory surrounding the lake is covered with forests.

Generally, both shorelines are quite regular. But the Michigan side is broken by Thunder Bay at Alpena and the larger Saginaw Bay at Saginaw.

Along the northern shore of the lake, North Channel is created by Manitoulin Island. This island separates North Channel from the main body of the lake. Eastward, beyond North Channel is Georgian Bay, the huge arm of Lake Huron.

Georgian Bay, the largest bay on Lake Huron, is about one hundred and twenty miles long and fifty miles wide. Its clear blue waters were the first portion of the Great Lakes to be seen by white men.

Lake Huron has more islands than any of the five Great Lakes. Its northern surface is dotted with many small islands.

One group, known as the Thirty Thousand Islands, is strewn across the northern half of Georgian Bay. Some are tiny, ranging from tree-covered spots to others of considerable size.

Some of the larger and more important islands of the lake are Cockburn, Drummond, St. Joseph, Bois Blanc, and Mackinac Islands.

Lake Huron not only has the greatest number of islands; it

Georgian Bay

contains the largest fresh-water island in the world. This is Manitoulin Island, a part of Canada. Isle Royale in Lake Superior is only a little more than one-third as large as Manitoulin Island.

Over eighty miles long with a width varying from two to about forty miles, its surface is dotted with dense forests and more than one hundred small lakes. Its coastline is rugged and very deeply indented all around.

The scenery of this region is considered by many to be the most beautiful and picturesque in the entire Great Lakes area. A boat trip through this island-strewn region is most delightful.

Within the last few years it has become a popular vacation site. Many cottages and hotels have been built here to add to the pleasure and comfort of visitors.

An air of mystery seems to hang over Manitoulin Island. The spell of the island invites those who have once been there to return again.

When white men came to the region, the Indians believed the island was the home of the Great Manitou of their tribes. They believed in many manitous or spirits. But this particular manitou was more powerful and stronger than all others.

In the Straits of Mackinac—the body of water connecting Lake Michigan and Lake Huron—is Mackinac Island. Indians called it Michilimackinac, which means Place of the Great Turtle. White men soon shortened this name to its more common form of Mackinac.

From the time of the early French explorers, this island has been important to the history of the region. It was the gathering place of Indians, the meeting place for fur traders, and the point where explorers paused to rest before continuing on their way.

Fort Mackinac

Old sailing vessel

At the end of the American Revolution, Mackinac Island became part of the United States. Yet it continued to be held and occupied by a British garrison. Finally with the signing of Jay's Treaty, England agreed to evacuate it in June, 1796. From that time it has remained under the control of the United States, except for a brief period during the War of 1812, when it was captured by the British. It is now part of Michigan.

Compared to some of the other islands, Mackinac is quite small. It is only three miles long and two miles wide. Its surface is rocky and wooded. Picturesque old Fort Mackinac with its blockhouses overlooking the water dominates the heights. It has been preserved as a reminder of the role it played in the history of this area.

Mackinac Island is now a state park. Automobiles are not permitted to operate here. Horses and buggies are available to visitors for a leisurely sightseeing drive around this old, historic island. Thus, the quaint atmosphere of the place has been retained. It is a popular vacation spot and is visited each year by hosts of tourists.

Much commerce moves on Lake Huron. Along with huge ore carriers, oil tankers play a very important role in present-day commerce. The first oil tanker made its appearance on the Great Lakes in 1910.

Because the lake serves as a connecting link between the upper and lower lakes, most of the commerce is through traffic from ports on Lakes Michigan and Superior to ports on Lake Erie. Iron ore, coal, grain, and limestone are the most important products moving through the lake.

Port Huron, on the St. Clair River, stretches for miles along

Oil tanker

the river and extends along Huron's shore. The city had its lumbering era and shipbuilding became important. Later, deposits of salt, oil, and natural gas were developed, helping the city to grow to its present size.

Thomas Edison, the inventor, came to live in Port Huron when he was seven years old. He spent his boyhood and early manhood there. It was in the basement of his father's house that he had his first laboratory.

When Edison was a young man, an ice jam in the St. Clair River snapped the cable connecting Port Huron and Sarnia, Ontario, across the river.

At the time, Edison was working for a railroad. He climbed aboard a locomotive, and using the long and short whistle blasts corresponding to the Morse Code, he began calling Sarnia.

Shrilly the whistle tooted, "Hello, Sarnia, do you get me?"

Edison made several attempts before his message was recognized in Sarnia and answered.

Port Huron and Sarnia are connected by the Blue Water International Bridge.

For the most part, Sarnia lies on the St. Clair River. The city is known for its oil refineries which are the most extensive in Canada.

Goderich, Ontario, is an important town on the eastern coast of Lake Huron. It is situated at the mouth of the Maitland River and is an important grain port. Other Canadian towns of importance are Owen Sound, Collingwood, and Midland.

Detroit is situated on the broad, deep Detroit River. A settlement was founded on the river bank in 1701 by Antoine de la Mothe Cadillac. From a very small beginning Detroit

Blue Water International Bridge

Detroit, Michigan

has grown to be one of the largest manufacturing cities of our country.

When it was a young, struggling city there was a great need all through the area for boats, wagons, buggies, and other vehicles. Its favorable situation made their manufacture possible, while nearby forests supplied the necessary lumber.

At the time the automobile was invented, many wagon, buggy, and boat shops were converted into automobile factories. In this way, Detroit was able to get an early start manufacturing automobiles.

Detroit has been called the Automobile Capital of the World. Necessary raw materials—iron ore, limestone, coal— are shipped into the city by the Great Lakes.

Finished products can be moved out by water, by railroad, and by highway.

Automobiles built in and around Detroit are sent not only to all parts of our country. They are to be found in all corners of the world.

Just across the Detroit River opposite Detroit is the Canadian City of Windsor. Detroit and Windsor are connected by bridge, tunnel, and ferry.

Windsor is one of Canada's busy industrial centers. This city has steel mills, chemical plants, and automobile factories.

The waters of Lake Huron empty into Lake Erie by way of the St. Clair River, Lake St. Clair, and the Detroit River. This long waterway between the two lakes is the third link in the chain of five lakes, and is one of the busiest marine highways in the world.

Sailing on Lake St. Clair

LAKE ERIE

Lake Erie is the fourth largest of the Great Lakes. It stretches from southwest to northeast between Lake Huron and Lake Ontario. It lies farther south than any of the other lakes.

The Canadian Province of Ontario borders the entire northern shore of Lake Erie. Its eastern and southern shores are bordered by New York, Pennsylvania, and Ohio. The greatest length of its shore is formed by Ohio, and on the west it is bounded by a small part of Michigan.

Lake Erie's elevation is five hundred and seventy-two feet above sea level. It is only slightly lower than Lake Huron. It is about two hundred and forty miles long and, at its greatest width the lake is fifty-eight miles across.

Geologists have said that Lake Erie is the oldest of the five Great Lakes. It is also the shallowest, having a maximum depth of only two hundred and ten feet.

Lake Erie is the most choppy and tempestuous of the five lakes. Due to its shallow basin it is quickly agitated by sudden gales. These windstorms sweep across the lake without warning, creating huge waves. This feature was noted by some of the early Europeans who traveled on its waters.

Lake Erie was the last of the Great Lakes to be discovered. Its existence might have been known earlier. But there were no reports of visits by white men until the year 1669. Then, Joliet and his Indian guide paddled along the northern coast of the lake to the outlet of the Grand River at Port Maitland.

At the beginning of the War of 1812, the British held con-

trol of Lake Erie, including the settlement at Detroit. Their defeat on the lake was one of the great victories of this war.

At Erie, Pennsylvania in the fall of 1812, work was started on several ships that were to make up part of Commodore Oliver Hazard Perry's fleet. The other part was waiting for him in Buffalo, New York.

When Perry reached the settlement of Erie in March, 1813, he proceeded at once to complete and outfit the ships for action.

His next task was to unite the two American units. He knew that Captain Barclay, commanding the British fleet, was lying in wait for him just off Buffalo.

Under cover of a heavy mantle of fog, Perry ran his ships out of Buffalo. He slipped past the British ships, sailed southwest, and joined his little squadron at Erie. He was then ready for action. He set out in his flagship, the "Lawrence," in search of the British fleet. About noon on September 10, 1813, the two fleets met at Put in Bay near Sandusky, Ohio.

Immediately the "Lawrence" engaged the "Detroit," Barclay's flagship. Soon Perry found the long-range fire of the British guns very destructive. He gave the order to move in closer to the enemy. Both fleets maneuvered about, pouring heavy fire into each other's ships.

Commodore Oliver Hazard Perry

The "Lawrence" suffered great damage. Her rigging was shot away; her guns were rendered useless. Many of the crew were killed, while others lay wounded on the deck; and she was obliged to drop from her position.

General William H. Harrison

Her sister ship, the "Niagara" now came forward. Perry lowered the only undamaged boat on the "Lawrence." With his battle flag in his arms, he was rowed to the "Niagara."

Once on board, he pressed her into action toward Barclay's line. Her guns opened up with a smashing volley, while Perry's new crew raked the decks of the "Detroit" with rifle and pistol shots.

The other American vessels were aiding in the attack from all sides.

Soon the flagship "Detroit" became completely disabled from the heavy American fire. Then Captain Barclay lowered his flags and his ships' guns ceased firing.

The American leader received the British captain on the blood-soaked deck of the "Lawrence" which was covered with dead and wounded men.

Perry accepted Barclay's surrender. Then on the back of an envelope he scribbled the message, "We have met the enemy and they are ours," and sent it to General Harrison commanding the Army forces on the Maumee River.

[59]

Both sides had suffered heavy losses in the battle. But Commodore Perry was now in command on Lake Erie.

With Lake Erie in American hands, General Harrison was able to move north and recapture Detroit. He drove the British across the Detroit River, defeating them in the Battle of the Thames River on October 5, 1813.

The shoreline of Lake Erie is very regular, except where it is broken by the Peninsula of Point Pelee and of Rondeau in the west and Long Point in the east.

Sandusky Bay is the largest and most important of the bays. Maumee Bay, Inner Bay of Long Point, and Outer Bay of Long Point are other indentations along the shore.

A number of islands are grouped in the western section of the lake north of Sandusky, Ohio. North Bass, Middle Bass, South Bass, Pelee, Kelleys, and Green Islands are the largest.

The first steamboat to appear on Lake Erie was the "Walk-in-the-Water." She was a side-wheeler, having been launched in the Niagara River in 1818.

She started out on her maiden voyage on August 23 and created quite a sensation around the lake. Her first run was to Detroit and back, stopping at Dunkirk, Erie, and Cleveland.

In whatever port she entered she was enthusiastically received. Whole towns came down to the waterfront to watch the arrival of this first steamboat. A salute from a cannon on her deck announced her arrival.

On her final trip for the season of 1821, she struck a sudden gale a few miles west of Buffalo, New York. All night she was badly whipped about by the gale. Her seams were opened, allowing water to pour in.

At daybreak a lifeline was secured to a point on shore and the passengers and crew reached safety in the ship's boat.

Cleveland, Ohio

Docks at Ashtabula, Ohio

Unlike the southern shore of Lake Erie, which is a beehive of activity, the northern or Canadian shore is very quiet. Here there are no large cities, but many towns.

Along the southern coast are many large manufacturing cities, where great and varied industries flourish. Some factories and mills turn out quantities of steel, flour, paper, automobiles, and other manufactured products.

Four of the seven major ports of the Great Lakes are located in this region: Buffalo at the eastern end of the lake, Detroit near the western end of the lake on the Detroit River, and Toledo and Cleveland on the Ohio shore.

Other prominent cities along the shores of Lake Erie are Erie in Pennsylvania, Conneaut, Ashtabula, Lorain, and Sandusky in Ohio.

On October 26, 1825, the Erie Canal was opened. It connected Lake Erie with the Hudson River at Albany, thus making it possible to ship goods from Lake Erie to the Atlantic Ocean.

On that fall day a canal boat, the "Seneca Chief," set out from Buffalo for Sandy Hook in New York Harbor. It was towed by mules walking slowly along the towpath; and carried DeWitt Clinton, the great canal builder, and other notable passengers.

As the boat passed through towns and cities along the canal it was greeted with wild acclaim. Bands played, church bells rang, and cannons boomed their salutes. Other boats joined in a gay procession behind the "Seneca Chief."

Also on board the canal boat was a cask of fresh water from Lake Erie. When the boat finally reached its destination, the water was emptied into New York Harbor with a fine ceremony.

On the return trip the "Seneca Chief" carried a cask of

Old Erie Canal

salt water from the ocean. This time it was emptied into Lake Erie, thus completing the symbolic union of the Great Lakes and the Atlantic Ocean.

The Erie Canal soon became a main artery for immigrants to the new West; and carried huge quantities of goods from Lake Erie to the East. By 1900 a much deeper, wider waterway had to be dug. Some years later, the New York State Barge Canal came into being. It was first used in 1918. A variety of heavy products, including coal, lumber, and grain are now carried by large, flat-bottomed barges.

Fishing is a very important industry on Lake Erie and Sandusky is the leading fishing port. The catch includes herring, pike, whitefish, and trout.

In well-equipped fish houses the fish are rapidly sorted, cleaned, and prepared for market. This work is done by machine.

Ice-fishing in winter is popular. As soon as the ice is thick enough and strong enough to support the weight of a man, fishermen drag their shanties far out on the lake.

These shanties are made of light-weight wood and are about four feet square. They are just big enough for one person to sit in comfortably. They have a door and a couple of small windows, and in the floor is a large hole.

The shanties are mounted on sled runners so that they can be easily pushed about.

When the fishermen go out for a day, they take a small wood or charcoal stove with fuel, and whatever else they will use: food, bait, fishing tackle. They cut a large hole through the thick ice to the water, then slide their shanties into place over the ice hole. In this way they can see the fish swimming below.

Welland Canal

Buffalo, New York

Although ice-fishing is mostly commercial, there are many sportsmen who love to follow this winter sport.

The only natural waterway between Lake Erie and Lake Ontario is the Niagara River. Because of the rapids and the great Niagara Falls in the river, it is useless as a commercial waterway.

To permit passage between these two lower lakes, the Welland Ship Canal was constructed on the Canadian side of the Niagara River. It is cut across the narrow isthmus between the lakes.

The Canal is a very important link in the Great Lakes-St. Lawrence Waterway. It connects Port Colborne, Ontario, on Lake Erie with Port Weller, Ontario, on Lake Ontario. Nearly twenty-eight miles long, it runs parallel to the Niagara River.

The first canal was opened in 1829. It has been widened and deepened since that time. Finally, in 1931, the new Welland Ship Canal was completed. It is the fourth and last link in the chain of Great Lakes.

The Canal is remarkable in that it lifts and lowers ships about three hundred and twenty-six feet, or the difference in elevation between Lake Erie and Lake Ontario.

This is accomplished by a series of locks. Each lock has a lift of about forty-six feet. The locks are eight hundred feet long, eighty feet wide, and about thirty feet deep.

Through this Canal pass enormous tonnages of iron ore, grain, coal, pulp, oil, and manufactured products. It is large enough to accommodate the biggest ships and freighters that navigate on the Great Lakes.

At one time, before this part of our country became covered with its present network of railroads, several canals connected Lake Erie with different cities. Today, only the Welland Canal and the New York State Barge Canal still handle Lake Erie commerce.

New York State Barge Canal

LAKE ONTARIO

Lake Ontario is the smallest of the Great Lakes. It is believed that at one time the lake was considerably larger and deeper than it is today.

It is the most easterly of the five-link chain of lakes. The northern, western, and southwestern shores of the lake are bounded by the Canadian Province of Ontario. Its eastern and southeastern shores are bounded by the State of New York.

From east to west the greatest length of Lake Ontario is about one hundred and ninety-three miles. The greatest width from north to south is fifty-three miles.

Lake Ontario lies at an elevation of about two hundred and forty-six feet above sea level. Its elevation is lower than all four other Great Lakes.

As one of the deeper of the five lakes, it has a maximum depth of over seven hundred feet. Because the lake is so deep, most of it lies below sea level; thus, the deep water remains unmoved by surface winds and currents.

Lake Ontario was discovered by Etienne Brule in 1615. He is said to have visited the western end of the lake while he was living with the Indians. But he did not leave any written records of his wanderings and discoveries. When Champlain learned about the lake from Brule, he came to the region to explore.

The Falls at Niagara are a natural barrier in the Niagara River that connects Lake Erie with Lake Ontario. Tons of water plunge over the Falls, dropping one hundred and sixty-seven feet to the river below. They are a spectacle to behold.

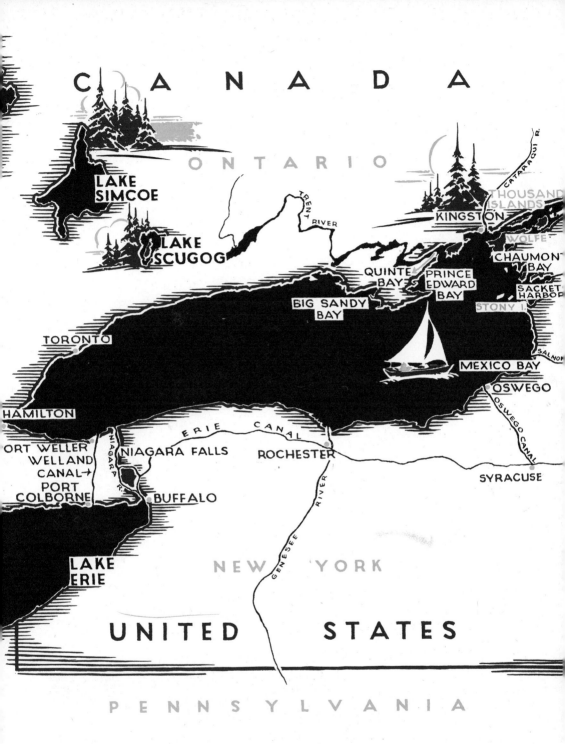

LAKE ONTARIO

Both the Canadian and American Falls are visited and photographed more than any other scenic wonder in America. Many tourists from both sides of the International Border are attracted to this region, making it a very popular vacation spot.

After the river plunges over the Falls, it continues on its turbulent way through the gorge, finally entering Lake Ontario.

The shoreline around the lake is generally unbroken. But at the eastern end there are several indentations, Sackets Harbor Bay, Chaumont Bay, and Mexico Bay.

On the northern shore Big Sandy, Quinte, and Prince Edward Bays are the largest. Prince Edward Peninsula extends out into Lake Ontario for a considerable distance.

Free of islands at the western end, the northeastern section of the lake is dotted with them. Amherst, Stony, and Wolfe Islands being a few of the most important.

Some of the chief rivers flowing into Lake Ontario from the New York side are the Genesee, Oswego, Salmon, and

Niagara Falls

Black. From the Canadian shore the Trent is the largest.

Because of moderate temperatures around the lake, an important fruit-growing region has developed.

Although the fruit belt extends on both sides of the boundary between Canada and the United States, it is of far greater significance to Canada.

Many regions in the two countries are well adapted to

Picking Apples

raising fruit. But from this district comes Canada's main fruit supply. Therefore this area is of the greatest importance to her.

Cherries, peaches, plums, pears, and grapes are grown in abundance. Apples in particular are raised in great quantities and rank as the most important crop.

Here the chief industries are connected with fruit and fruit preserving in various forms.

Commerce on Lake Ontario is much more limited than it is anywhere else on the Great Lakes. Until the Welland Canal was built, Lake Ontario was cut off from the other lakes. Even after the Canal was opened, the lake remained somewhat apart, for the St. Lawrence River meets most of Canada's shipping needs.

Grain, coal, and lumber are the chief cargoes carried on Lake Ontario.

Shortly after the War of 1812, two small steamboats, the "Ontario" and "Frontenac," were built and operated on Lake Ontario.

Many pleasure boats now ply the waters of the lake. Scenic trips along the coast and among the Thousand Islands of the St. Lawrence River are very popular with tourists.

During the winter season the lake does not completely freeze over. Ice forms in harbors and in shallow water along the shores.

The entire length of the lake can be navigated at all times of the year, but harbors are closed from December to April.

Along the New York shore the only cities of importance are Oswego and Rochester. Most of the New York coastline is bordered by small fruit farms and dotted with summer resorts and summer homes.

Oswego is the most easterly of the United States ports on Lake Ontario. Between the port and Syracuse is a spur of the New York State Barge Canal. The spur, one hundred and ninety-four miles long, connects Oswego with Albany on the Hudson River.

Oswego is a manufacturing city. It produces shades, shade cloth, Venetian blinds, textiles, paper, paper bags and boxes, matches, machinery and foundry articles.

Rochester, whose outskirts extend to the lake's coast, is situated on the Erie Canal. It is one of the liveliest and busiest cities in this region.

At one time, Rochester was a great flour-milling center and was nicknamed the Flour City. Although flour is still milled here, it is no longer as important an industry as it formerly was.

Today, Rochester is noted for its nursery business. Optical instruments, cameras and photographic supplies, clothing, and

Genessee Falls, Rochester, New York

Hydro-Electric Plant on Niagara River

shoes, are among some of the other important items manufactured here.

Along the Canadian shore of Lake Ontario lies one of the most densely populated regions in Canada; many cities have grown up here. Three of the largest and most important are Kingston, Toronto, and Hamilton.

Hamilton is at the extreme western tip or head of the lake. Situated on a large, land-locked lagoon, it has a spacious harbor. The Burlington Channel connects it with the main body of the lake.

Hamilton is a manufacturing center. Iron, steel, agricultural implements, shoes, clothing, and furniture are among some of the items manufactured there.

It is the center of Canada's iron and steel industries and has been called the Birmingham of Canada.

Because of its location in the fruit belt, Hamilton has become a great shipping point for fruits and vegetables. The city has a huge public market, said to be one of the largest in the world.

As early as 1720, a fort was built on the site of present-day Toronto, but it was abandoned in a few years. Then in 1749, a French trading post, Fort Rouille, was founded on the same site.

The name Toronto is a Huron Indian word meaning The Place of Meeting.

Toronto is the capital and largest city of Ontario, and a bustling commercial and industrial center. Its harbor is one of the best on the Great Lakes.

The city has an abundance of hydro-electric power which it uses for manufacturing purposes.

Toronto

Toronto is an important railroad center. The downtown area of the city is noted for its modern buildings and skyscrapers. Visitors enter the city by railroad, steamer, automobile, and plane.

One of Canada's main livestock markets is in Toronto. Some of its industries are shipbuilding, the manufacture of paints, machinery, automobiles, shoes, and clothing. During World War II its factories turned out huge quantities of ammunition and fighting equipment.

Fort Frontenac was built in 1673 on the site of the present city of Kingston, Ontario. During the War of 1812, Kingston was an important fortress and the chief British naval base on Lake Erie.

It is situated at the mouth of the Cataragui River at the junction of Lake Ontario and the St. Lawrence River. The city has a spacious harbor with shipyards and drydocks.

Kingston is connected with Ottawa City and the Ottawa River by the Rideau Canal, a distance of one hundred and twenty-six miles.

A small canal, it was at one time more important than at present. Railroads now move most of the traffic in and out of the city.

Locomotives and ships are built here. The city also has woolen mills, and nylon and paper box factories.

It is also the gateway to the Thousand Islands. These islands in the St. Lawrence River have long been famous for their beauty. Many are used for summer homes. The area is a favorite vacation land and attracts visitors from both Canada and the United States.

Lake Ontario empties its waters through the St. Lawrence River into the Atlantic Ocean.

Thousand Islands

At the point where the river issues from Lake Ontario, it is about two and one-half miles wide. Throughout most of its course to the Atlantic Ocean, the river maintains a width of about two miles. From Quebec northeastward, the St. Lawrence begins to widen.

By the time it reaches the Gulf of St. Lawrence, it has broadened out to about ninety miles. The St. Lawrence is the largest river in northeastern North America.

Jacques Cartier discovered and named the Gulf of St. Lawrence in 1534. On his second voyage in 1535 and 1536, he explored farther and discovered the St. Lawrence River.

Like other French explorers, he sought a passage to China. He continued his explorations, finally landing at the site now occupied by the city of Quebec. From here he continued in-

Quebec

CANADA

QUEBEC

GULF OF ST. LAWRENCE

ANTICOSTI

GASPE PENINSULA

PRINCE EDWARD ISLAND

NEW BRUNSWICK

NOVA SCOTIA

QUEBEC

MAINE

ST. LAWRENCE RIVER

ONTARIO

OTTAWA RIVER

MONTREAL

OTTAWA

LAKE CHAMPLAIN

KINGSTON

THOUSAND ISLANDS

LAKE ONTARIO

UNITED STATES

ATLANTIC OCEAN

From Lake Ontario to the sea

land until he arrived at the little Indian village of Hochelaga on the site of present-day Montreal.

In the early days of exploration and pioneering, the St. Lawrence River was the water highway used by fur traders, explorers, and colonists as they pushed westward.

The Great Lakes-St. Lawrence Waterway System provides an excellent shipping lane for ocean-going ships hauling cargoes from such distant lands as Norway, Sweden, and Holland.

Goods from as far inland as Duluth, Minnesota or from any other Great Lakes ports can be shipped to any ports in the world.

The Great Lakes with their rivers and canals with locks combine with the St. Lawrence River to form the world's greatest inland waterway.